Bible Christmas Story for Kids

The timeless nativity story retold in a gentle, engaging way that helps children understand the true meaning of Christmas

SPARK CRAFTER

TABLE OF CONTENTS

INTRODUCTION

The Greatest Gift of All

Dear young readers and families,

Welcome to a very special journey through one of the most beloved stories in the Bible – the birth of Jesus Christ. As we open the pages of this book together, we're about to embark on an adventure that has touched the hearts of millions of people around the world for over two thousand years.

A Story That Changed the World

The Christmas story isn't just any tale. It's a story that has the power to fill our hearts with wonder, joy, and hope. It's a story about how God's love for us is so big, so amazing, that He sent His own Son to be born as a tiny baby in a humble stable. Can you imagine that? The King of Kings, coming to Earth not in a golden chariot or a magnificent palace, but as a small, helpless infant in a manger!

This incredible event happened long ago in a little town called Bethlehem, but its message continues to echo through time, touching lives in every corner of the world. People of all ages, from different countries and cultures, celebrate Christmas because of this very story we're about to explore together.

More Than Just a Holiday

You might be wondering, "Why is this story so important?" Well, the birth of Jesus is much more than just the reason we have a holiday called Christmas. It's the beginning of God's amazing plan to show His love for every single person on Earth – including you!

In the pages that follow, you'll meet some extraordinary characters:

- Mary, a young woman chosen by God for a very special purpose
- Joseph, a kind and faithful man who trusted in God's plan
- Shepherds, who received an incredible surprise while watching their sheep

- Wise Men, who traveled from far away, following a bright star
- And of course, baby Jesus, the most important baby ever born

As we journey through their experiences, we'll discover some important themes that are at the heart of the Christmas story:

- Faith: Believing in God's promises, even when they seem impossible
- Humility: Understanding that true greatness often comes in small packages
- Love: Experiencing the incredible love God has for each one of us

A Message of Hope and Salvation

The birth of Jesus wasn't just a happy event – it was the beginning of something much bigger. You see, God sent Jesus to Earth with a very special mission: to grow up and teach people about God's love, and ultimately to offer the gift of salvation to everyone.

Salvation might sound like a big word, but it simply means being saved or rescued. In this case, Jesus came to rescue us from the things that separate us from God, like the mistakes we make (which the Bible calls "sin"). His birth was the first step in God's plan to bring us close to Him and to give us the chance to live forever in Heaven.

A Story for Everyone

Whether you've heard the Christmas story many times before or this is your very first time, there's always something new to discover. As you read, you might find yourself imagining what it was like to be there on that very first Christmas night. How would you have felt if you were a shepherd seeing angels in the sky? Or a Wise Man following a mysterious star?

Remember, this story isn't just for grownups or for people who go to church. It's for everyone, including kids just like you! God's love is so big that it includes every person, no matter how young or old, rich or poor, or where they come from.

An Invitation to Wonder

As we begin this journey through the Christmas story, I invite you to open your heart and your imagination.

Let yourself be filled with wonder at the miracles that happened that night in Bethlehem. Think about how a tiny baby born in such a humble place could bring so much hope and joy to the whole world.

Most importantly, as you read about God's incredible gift of Jesus, remember that this gift is for you too. The same love that came down to Earth that first Christmas night is still here today, waiting for you to unwrap it and make it part of your own life story.

So, are you ready to step back in time and witness the greatest birth in history? Let's turn the page and begin our adventure into the true meaning of Christmas – a celebration of God's love and the beginning of His wonderful plan for all of us.

Merry Christmas, and may the joy of this story fill your heart today and always!

CHAPTER 1: THE PROPHECIES OF THE MESSIAH

A very long time ago, even before Jesus was born, God made some very special promises to His people. These promises were like clues in a wonderful treasure hunt, telling people about a special King who would come one day to save everyone. Let's discover how God told His people about baby Jesus long before He was born!

There was a man named Isaiah who loved God very much. God gave Isaiah special messages about the coming King, who would be called the Messiah. Isaiah was like God's messenger, telling everyone the exciting news!

"Listen, everyone!" Isaiah would say with joy. "God has told me that a special baby will be born! He will be called Wonderful Counselor, Mighty God, Everlasting Father, Prince of Peace!"

The people would gather around to hear more. Children would sit with wide eyes as Isaiah told them about the promises.

Another one of God's messengers was named Micah. He had an important message too! God told Micah exactly where the special baby would be born - in a little town called Bethlehem.

"Even though Bethlehem is a small town," Micah announced, "something big will happen there! The Messiah will be born in Bethlehem!"

Years and years passed. Grandparents told their children, who told their children, about these wonderful promises. They waited and waited, keeping hope in their hearts. Some people wondered when God's promises would come true. But the wise ones remembered that God always keeps His promises, even if it takes a long time.

God sent more messengers with more clues:

- The Messiah would come from the family of King David
- He would bring peace and joy to the world
- He would be born to a young woman
- He would be a light to all people

It was like God was painting a picture, adding one color at a time, showing what the Messiah would be like. The people held these promises close to their hearts, like precious treasures.

Many years later, when the time was just right, something amazing happened. All these promises started coming true! God hadn't forgotten a single one. Just like when you plant a seed and wait patiently for it to grow, God's promises grew into the most wonderful gift ever - baby Jesus!

Lesson: God always keeps His promises, even if we have to wait. Just like the people long ago waited for Jesus, we can trust that God will do what He says He will do.

Fun Activities for Kids:

- **Promise Tree:** Draw a tree and write God's promises about Jesus on paper leaves
- **Time Capsule Game:** Put small items in a box that remind you of God's promises
- **Prophet's Message:** Practice telling the good news like Isaiah and Micah

Discussion Questions:

- How do you feel when you have to wait for something special?
- What promises did God make about baby Jesus?
- Why do you think God gave so many clues about Jesus before He was born?
- How can we trust God's promises today?

Memory Verse:

"For unto us a child is born, unto us a son is given" - Isaiah 9:6

Creative Prayer:

Dear God, thank you for always keeping your promises. Help us to be patient and trust you, just like the people who waited for Jesus. Amen.

Fun Facts Corner:

- Isaiah lived about 700 years before Jesus was born!
- Bethlehem means "House of Bread" in Hebrew
- The prophecies about Jesus are like pieces of a puzzle that all fit together perfectly

Family Activity:

Make a "Promise Calendar" leading up to Christmas. Each day, open a paper door to find one of God's promises about Jesus written inside. This helps us understand how the people felt waiting for the Messiah!

CHAPTER 2: THE ANNUNCIATION TO MARY

In a small town called Nazareth, there lived a young woman named Mary. She was kind and gentle, and she loved God with all her heart. Mary lived a simple life, helping her family and getting ready to marry a carpenter named Joseph.

One ordinary day, something extraordinary happened that would change the world forever!

Mary was going about her daily tasks when suddenly, a bright light filled the room. There, standing before her, was a beautiful angel named Gabriel! His appearance was so magnificent that Mary felt a little scared.

"Don't be afraid, Mary," Gabriel said with a gentle voice. "God has chosen you for something very special. You have found favor with God!"

Mary listened with wonder as Gabriel continued to speak.

"You will have a baby boy," the angel announced, "and you shall name Him Jesus. He will be very special because He will be God's own Son! He will be great, and His kingdom will never end!"

Mary's heart beat faster as she heard these amazing words. She had so many questions! After all, she wasn't even married yet.

"How can this be?" Mary asked the angel.

Gabriel explained that this would be a miracle from God. "The Holy Spirit will come upon you," he said. "Nothing is impossible with God! Even your cousin Elizabeth, who everyone thought was too old to have children, is going to have a baby too!"

Mary had a choice to make. This was such big news! It would change everything in her life. Some people might not understand. It wouldn't be easy. But Mary's faith in God was strong, and she trusted that God's plan was good.

With a humble heart full of faith, Mary replied, "I am the Lord's servant. Let everything happen just as you have said."

And just like that, the angel Gabriel departed, leaving Mary with the most wonderful secret in the world. She was going to be the mother of God's Son! Her heart was filled with joy and wonder at how God had chosen her, a simple young woman, to be part of His amazing plan.

Lesson: When God asks us to do something special, we can trust Him like Mary did, even if it seems scary or difficult. God chooses ordinary people for extraordinary purposes!

Interactive Elements:

Story Discussion Questions:

- How do you think Mary felt when she first saw the angel?
- What made Mary's answer to Gabriel so special?
- When have you had to trust God with something that seemed scary?
- How can we show faith like Mary did?

Activities for Learning:

Angel Gabriel's Message Box

- Create a special box with golden paper
- Write God's promises on small scrolls to put inside
- Take turns being Gabriel and delivering the message to Mary

Trust Walk Game

- One child wears a blindfold
- Another child guides them safely through a simple obstacle course
- Discuss how this relates to trusting God's guidance

Mary's Journal Entry

Pretend to be Mary and write or draw about the day the angel visited

Share your thoughts about how she might have felt

Songs to Sing Together:

🎵 Mary's Song 🎵

(To the tune of "Twinkle, Twinkle, Little Star")

CopyMary trusted God above,

Showing faith and showing love.

When the angel came to say,

"God has chosen you today!"

Mary said, "I'll do God's will,"

Teaching us to trust Him still.

Prayer Activity:

Make a "Trust Prayer Jar":

- Write down things you need to trust God with
- Decorate the jar with stars and angels
- Pull one out each day to pray about

Memory Verse:

"For nothing will be impossible with God." - Luke 1:37

Fun Facts:

- Nazareth was a very small town
- Angels appear in many important Bible stories
- Gabriel's name means "God is my strength"
- Mary was probably a teenager when the angel visited her

Family Challenge:

This week, share times when you needed to trust God. Make a family "Trust Tree" by writing these experiences on paper leaves and adding them to a drawn tree trunk.

Remember: Just like Mary, we can trust God's plans for us, even when they surprise us or seem too big. God is always faithful!

CHAPTER 3: JOSEPH'S DREAM

In the town of Nazareth lived a kind and honest carpenter named Joseph. He worked hard in his workshop, crafting things from wood with his skilled hands. Joseph was engaged to marry Mary, and he was very happy about their future together.

But one day, Joseph learned something that made his heart very heavy. Mary was going to have a baby, and he didn't understand how this could be. Joseph knew he wasn't the father, and he felt very confused and sad.

Joseph was a good man with a gentle heart. He didn't want to hurt Mary or make people say unkind things about her. While others might have been angry, Joseph thought carefully about what to do. He decided he would quietly end their engagement so Mary wouldn't be embarrassed.

That night, as Joseph lay sleeping on his bed, something amazing happened! God sent a special messenger – an angel – to speak to him in a dream.

"Joseph, son of David," the angel said in a clear, strong voice, "don't be afraid to take Mary as your wife. The baby she is carrying is very, very special. This baby is from the Holy Spirit!"

The angel continued with wonderful news: "Mary will have a son, and you must name Him Jesus, because He will save His people from their sins. This is all happening just as God promised long ago!"

When Joseph woke up, he felt different. All his worries had melted away like morning dew in the sunshine. He understood now that God had chosen both him and Mary for something extraordinary. This baby would be the Savior that God had promised!

Without hesitating, Joseph did exactly what the angel had told him to do. He went to Mary and told her that he understood everything now. He would stay by her side and help take care of God's special baby. Joseph would be Jesus's earthly father, teaching Him how to be a carpenter and showing Him how to be kind and good.

Mary was so happy that Joseph believed her and trusted God's plan. Together, they would prepare for the amazing gift God was giving to the world through them.

Lesson: Sometimes God asks us to trust Him even when things don't make sense at first. Like Joseph, we can choose to be brave and follow God's plan, knowing that He always has a good reason for what He asks us to do.

Interactive Activities:

1. Dream Pillowcase Craft:

- Decorate a paper pillowcase with angels and stars
- Write "God speaks to those who listen" on it
- Use it to retell Joseph's dream story

2. Carpenter's Corner:

- Set up a pretend carpenter's workshop
- Use wooden blocks or safe tools to build things
- Talk about how Joseph might have taught Jesus to be a carpenter

3. Trust Walk Game:

- Create a simple obstacle course

- One child leads another who's blindfolded
- Discuss how Joseph had to trust God without seeing the whole plan

Discussion Questions:

- Why was Joseph worried at first?
- How did God help Joseph understand His plan?
- What made Joseph special as Jesus's earthly father?
- How can we trust God when we don't understand everything?

Role-Play Activity: "Joseph's Choice"

- Scene 1: Joseph in his workshop, thinking about what to do
- Scene 2: The angel's visit in the dream
- Scene 3: Joseph telling Mary he understands now

Memory Verse Game:

"When Joseph woke up, he did what the angel of the Lord had commanded him." - Matthew 1:24

(Make it into a fun action game where children "sleep" and "wake up" to say the verse)

Character Qualities We Learn from Joseph:

- Kindness - He didn't want to hurt Mary
- Patience - He thought carefully before acting
- Obedience - He followed God's instructions
- Trust - He believed God's message
- Courage - He did the right thing even though it was hard

Family Discussion Starters:

- Talk about times when you had to trust God's plan
- Share stories of when something difficult turned out to be good
- Discuss how we can show kindness like Joseph did

Creative Prayer Activity:

Make a "Trust Tree":

- Draw a large tree on paper
- Write prayers on leaf shapes
- Add new leaves when God answers prayers

Fun Learning Games:

1. "Joseph's Workshop"

Materials needed:

- Building blocks
- Play tools
- Work apron

Let children pretend to be Joseph in his workshop, building things while talking about the story.

2. "Angel's Message Relay"

- Children line up in teams
- Whisper the angel's message down the line
- See how accurately the message is delivered

3. "Dream Stars"

- Cut out star shapes
- Write parts of the story on each star
- Have children put them in order while retelling the story

Bedtime Prayer:

Dear God,

Help us to be like Joseph,

Brave and kind and true.

When we don't understand things,

Help us trust in You.

Amen.

Take-Home Challenge:

This week, when something seems difficult or confusing:

- Remember Joseph's story
- Take a moment to pray
- Trust that God has a plan
- Be kind like Joseph was

Remember: Just as Joseph trusted God's surprising plan, we can trust that God knows what's best for us, even when things seem unexpected or confusing!

CHAPTER 4: THE JOURNEY TO BETHLEHEM

In the town of Nazareth, Mary and Joseph were preparing for a very important journey. The Roman emperor had made a new rule: everyone had to travel to their family's hometown to be counted in something called a census. For Joseph, this meant traveling to Bethlehem, the city of his ancestors.

This wasn't going to be an easy trip. Mary was expecting baby Jesus soon, and Bethlehem was very far away – about 90 miles! That's like walking from one end of a big city to another... four times!

"Don't worry, Mary," Joseph said kindly. "God will watch over us." He helped Mary climb onto their gentle donkey, who would carry her during the long journey.

The path ahead was challenging. Sometimes it went up steep hills, and sometimes down into valleys. The sun was hot during the day, and the nights were cold. Mary and Joseph had to carry everything they needed: food, water, and blankets for camping.

"Are you comfortable?" Joseph would ask Mary often, making sure she was okay.

"Yes," Mary would answer with a brave smile. "God gives me strength when I'm tired."

Along the way, they met other travelers heading to their own hometowns. Some shared their food and water, showing how God sends help through kind people. When they needed rest, they would stop under shady trees or sleep under the stars at night.

They traveled for many days. Sometimes the donkey would go "hee-haw!" as if encouraging them to keep going. Joseph walked beside them, leading the way and watching for any dangers.

"Look!" said Mary one afternoon, pointing ahead. "I can see Bethlehem on that hill!"

The sight of the little town gave them new energy. Even though they were tired from their long journey, their hearts were full of joy. They had made it safely, just as God had planned!

Lesson: Just like Mary and Joseph, we can trust God when things are difficult. He helps us through long journeys and hard times, often sending help through kind people we meet along the way.

Interactive Activities:

1. "Journey Map Game":

Create a board game showing the path from Nazareth to Bethlehem

- Roll dice to move forward
- Land on spaces with challenges and blessings
- Learn about perseverance and trust

2. "Pack Your Travel Bag":

Children decide what to pack for the journey:

- Water bottle for thirst
- Snacks for hunger
- Blanket for cold
- Discussion about what's really important

3. "Walking with Faith":

A physical activity where children:

- Walk a path with safe obstacles
- Help each other like Mary and Joseph
- Learn about working together

Discussion Questions:

- Why did Mary and Joseph have to go to Bethlehem?
- What made their journey difficult?
- How did God help them along the way?
- What can we learn from their faith and courage?

Songs to Learn:

🎵 The Journey Song 🎵

(To the tune of "The Wheels on the Bus")

CopyMary and Joseph walked so far,

Walked so far, walked so far,

Mary and Joseph walked so far,

All the way to Bethlehem!

(Add verses about the donkey, the stars, etc.)

Craft Ideas:

1. "Journey Scroll":

- Long paper rolled like a scroll
- Draw different parts of the journey
- Add stickers for stars and animals
- Write encouraging words

2. "Donkey Friend":

- Paper bag puppet
- Googly eyes
- Grey yarn for mane
- Talk about how the donkey helped Mary

3. "Star Light Guide":

- Make paper star lanterns
- Add battery tea lights
- Remember God's guidance

Movement Activities:

1. "Journey Exercise":

- Walk in place (traveling)
- Climb imaginary hills (challenges)
- Rest under trees (God's care)
- Wave to other travelers (friendship)

2. "Helper Relay":

Teams work together to:

- Carry supplies
- Help friends over obstacles
- Share resources
- Reach the "Bethlehem" finish line

Prayer Activity:

Create a "Journey Prayer Journal":

- Draw pictures of your own journey
- Write thank you notes to God
- Share prayers for others on difficult journeys

Take-Home Activities:

1. "Stars of Promise":

- Cut out paper stars
- Write God's promises on them
- Hang them up as reminders

2. "Kind Traveler Cards":

- Make cards for people on journeys
- Share encouragement
- Be helpers like those Mary and Joseph met

Family Challenge:

During the week:

- Talk about difficult things you face
- Remember Mary and Joseph's journey
- Thank God for His help
- Look for ways to help others

Memory Verse:

"I can do all things through Christ who strengthens me." - Philippians 4:13

Bedtime Chat Questions:

- What journey did you take today?
- How did God help you?
- Who did you help along the way?
- What journey might you face tomorrow?

Remember: God is with us on every journey, just like He was with Mary and Joseph. When things get hard, we can trust Him to help us keep going!

CHAPTER 5: THE BIRTH OF JESUS

The little town of Bethlehem was very crowded. People had come from all over for the Roman census, filling every house and inn. Among them were Mary and Joseph, tired from their long journey from Nazareth.

"Please," Joseph asked at each inn, "do you have any room? My wife is about to have a baby."

But everywhere they went, they heard the same answer: "Sorry, we're full!"

Finally, one kind innkeeper saw how tired Mary was. "I don't have any rooms left," he said, "but you can stay in my stable. At least it will be warm and dry."

The stable was a simple place where animals lived. There were cows that said "moo," sheep that said "baa," and a gentle donkey that had carried Mary all the way from Nazareth. Fresh hay covered the floor, and the animals watched curiously as Joseph helped Mary get comfortable.

That night, something wonderful happened! Mary's baby was born – but this wasn't just any baby. This was Jesus, God's own Son! Mary wrapped Him snugly in soft cloths called swaddling clothes and laid Him in a manger. A manger was usually used to hold food for the animals, but tonight it became the first cradle for the King of Kings.

The cows and sheep and donkey gathered close, their gentle breath helping to keep baby Jesus warm. The stable was filled with peace and joy. There were no fancy decorations, no beautiful furniture, just simple surroundings filled with love.

Mary and Joseph looked at their newborn baby with wonder. They knew this tiny child was God's greatest gift to the world. Jesus, the Savior that God had promised so long ago, had finally come! And He came not to a palace or a fancy house, but to a humble stable, showing that God's love is for everyone, rich or poor.

The stars twinkled brightly that night, especially one very special star that shone right above the stable. It was as if all of heaven was celebrating the birth of Jesus!

Lesson: God often chooses simple and humble places for His most amazing miracles. Jesus being born in a stable shows us that wonderful things can happen anywhere, and that God's love is for everyone!

Interactive Elements:

1. Stable Scene Craft:

Materials needed:

- Brown paper bags (for stable)
- Cotton balls (for sheep)
- Yellow paper (for hay)
- Craft sticks (for manger)
- Let children create their own nativity scene!

2. "No Room at the Inn" Activity:

- Set up "inns" (chairs) around the room
- Children walk while music plays
- When music stops, find an "inn"
- Discuss how Mary and Joseph might have felt

3. Sensory Story Experience:

- Feel real hay (or yellow yarn)
- Listen to animal sounds
- Smell cinnamon (like stable spices)
- Experience the story with all senses

Discussion Questions:

- Why do you think God chose a stable for Jesus to be born?
- How would you have helped Mary and Joseph if you were there?
- What makes a place special – fancy decorations or the love inside?
- How can we make room for Jesus in our lives today?

Songs to Sing:

🎵 The Stable Song 🎵

(To the tune of "Twinkle, Twinkle, Little Star")

CopyIn a stable, long ago,

Baby Jesus lay below.

Though no fancy bed had He,

King of Kings He'd grow to be.

In that humble stable there,

God showed how much He does care.

Act It Out!:

Characters needed:

- Mary and Joseph
- Innkeeper
- Animals
- Star holder
- Props:
- Blue cloth for Mary
- Toy tools for Joseph
- Animal masks
- Blanket for baby Jesus
- Cardboard box for manger

Prayer Activity:

Create a "Humble Heart Prayer":

- Draw a heart
- Write ways to show love like Jesus
- Pray to have a kind and humble heart

Fun Facts Corner:

- Bethlehem means "House of Bread"
- Shepherds kept their sheep near Bethlehem
- Mangers were made of wood or stone
- Swaddling clothes were like special baby blankets

Family Activities:

1. "Make Room for Jesus":

- Create a special place in your home
- Add something each day until Christmas
- Talk about making room in our hearts

2. "Stable Service":

- Help clean someone's room or yard
- Share toys or clothes with others
- Show God's love through humble service

3. "Star Light, Star Bright":

- Go stargazing as a family
- Talk about the special star
- Share hopes and dreams

Memory Verse:

"And she gave birth to her firstborn son and wrapped him in swaddling cloths and laid him in a manger, because there was no place for them in the inn." - Luke 2:7

Bedtime Reflection:

- What simple things made you happy today?
- How can you share God's love tomorrow?
- Thank God for His greatest gift, Jesus

Take-Home Messages:

- God's love can be found in simple places
- Everyone is special to God
- The best gifts don't need fancy wrapping
- Jesus came for all people

Remember: Just like the stable became the most special place in the world that night, any place can become special when it's filled with God's love!

CHAPTER 6: THE SHEPHERDS AND THE ANGELS

On the night Jesus was born, in the fields outside Bethlehem, shepherds were watching over their sheep. These weren't rich or famous people – they were ordinary workers who spent their nights protecting their fluffy flocks from wolves and bears.

The shepherds sat around a small fire, wrapped in warm cloaks to keep away the chill. Some were dozing, while others kept watch. Their sheep were snuggled together nearby, making soft bleating sounds in the quiet night.

Suddenly, something amazing happened! The dark night sky lit up with a brilliant light! An angel appeared, shining with God's glory! The shepherds were so scared they nearly fell over!

"Don't be afraid!" the angel said with a kind voice. "I bring you good news that will bring great joy to all people! Today in Bethlehem, a Savior has been born! He is Christ, the Lord. Here's how you will find Him: Look for a baby wrapped in soft cloths, lying in a manger."

Before the shepherds could catch their breath, something even more wonderful happened! The sky filled with thousands of angels – more than anyone could count! They were all praising God and singing:

"Glory to God in the highest heaven,

And peace on earth to those with whom God is pleased!"

The shepherds had never seen or heard anything so beautiful. The angels' song echoed across the hills, making the night more glorious than the brightest day.

When the angels returned to heaven, the shepherds looked at each other with excitement. "Let's go right now to Bethlehem!" they said. "We must see this wonderful thing God has told us about!"

They hurried into town, leaving their sheep safely together in the field. They looked in stables and barns until they found exactly what the angel had described –

a newborn baby lying in a manger, with Mary and Joseph nearby.

The shepherds knelt before baby Jesus, their hearts full of joy and wonder. They told Mary and Joseph about the angels and their beautiful song. Mary listened carefully and kept all these things in her heart.

Then the shepherds went back to their sheep, but they weren't quiet about what they had seen! They told everyone they met about the baby Jesus and the angels' visit. Everyone who heard their story was amazed!

Lesson: God chose simple shepherds to hear the wonderful news first, showing that Jesus came for everyone, not just important or wealthy people. When God speaks, the best response is to hurry to follow His direction, just like the shepherds did!

Interactive Activities:

1. "Night Sky Theatre":

Materials needed:

- Black paper
- Silver and gold stars
- Flashlights
- Create the night sky and act out the angels appearing!

2. "Shepherd's Quest":

A hide-and-seek game where children:

- Look for a baby doll in a manger
- Follow paper stars as clues
- Share the good news when they find "baby Jesus"

3. "Angel Choir":

Learn and sing this simple praise song:

🎵 The Angels' Song 🎵

(To the tune of "Are You Sleeping?")

CopyGlory, glory!

Peace on earth!

God is with us,

Through Jesus' birth.

Angels singing,

Shepherds seeing,

Christ is born!

Christ is born!

Dramatic Play Elements:

Make Simple Costumes:

- Shepherd robes (old sheets)
- Angel wings (cardboard and tinfoil)
- Sheep ears (paper headbands)
- Shepherd's staff (curved stick)

Role-Play Scenes:

- Shepherds watching their sheep
- Angels appearing
- Journey to Bethlehem
- Finding baby Jesus
- Telling others the good news

Discussion Questions:

- Why do you think God chose shepherds to hear the news first?
- How would you feel if angels appeared to you?

- What made the shepherds hurry to find Jesus?
- How can we share good news about Jesus today?

Sensory Activities:

- Feel sheep's wool (or cotton balls)
- Listen to nighttime sounds
- Make angel music with bells
- Create shepherd's snacks (dried fruit and nuts)

Craft Corner: "Shepherd's Staff Stories":

- Make shepherd's staffs from pipe cleaners
- Attach small papers with ways to share God's love
- Practice telling the Christmas story using the staff as a prop

Memory Verse Game:

"Glory to God in the highest heaven, and on earth peace to those on whom his favor rests." - Luke 2:14

(Create motions for each phrase)

Family Activities:

1. "Starlight Walk":

- Take a family walk at night
- Look at the stars
- Talk about how the shepherds felt

2. "Good News Sharing":

- Make cards telling about Jesus
- Share them with neighbors
- Be shepherds sharing the good news

3. "Angel Light Show":

- Use flashlights in a dark room
- Take turns being angels and shepherds
- Sing praise songs together

Prayer Station:

Create a "Shepherd's Prayer Corner" with:

- Soft pillows to kneel on
- Battery candles for light
- Prayer prompts about sharing God's love

Take-Home Challenges:

Be like the shepherds:

- Watch for God's messages

- Hurry to follow God's directions
- Tell others about Jesus

Be like the angels:

- Bring good news to others
- Praise God with joy
- Help others not to be afraid

Remember: Just as the shepherds were chosen to hear the good news first, God often speaks to those with humble hearts who are ready to listen and follow!

CHAPTER 7: THE WISE MEN AND THE STAR

Far away in the East, where the sun first rises each morning, lived some very special men called the Magi. They were wise men who studied the stars and ancient scrolls. Every night, they would climb to their tall towers and look at the twinkling lights in the sky.

One night, something extraordinary happened! They saw a new star, brighter and more beautiful than any they had ever seen before. These wise men knew this wasn't just any star – it was a special sign from God! According to their ancient scrolls, this star meant that a new King had been born in the land of the Jews.

"We must find this new King!" they decided. "We will follow the star and bring Him special gifts!"

The wise men packed for their long journey. They chose three very special presents:

- **Gold:** a gift fit for a king

- **Frankincense**: a sweet-smelling incense used in worship
- **Myrrh**: a precious perfume

They loaded their camels with food, water, and supplies. The journey would be very long – across deserts, over mountains, and through valleys. But they didn't mind. They knew finding this special King was worth every step!

Day after day, they traveled. When the sun was hot, they rested in the shade. At night, they followed the bright star that seemed to lead them forward. Sometimes they joined caravans of other travelers, sharing stories around campfires under the starry sky.

Finally, they reached Jerusalem, the big city of the Jews. "Where is the newborn King?" they asked everyone they met. "We have seen His star and have come to worship Him!"

Their questions reached King Herod, who became worried about a new king. His wise men told him the Messiah was to be born in Bethlehem. So the Magi continued their journey, following the star until it stopped right above the house where Jesus was!

When they saw Jesus with Mary, they fell to their knees in worship. Their long journey had been worth every step! They opened their treasure chests and presented their special gifts to Jesus.

That night, God warned the wise men in a dream not to go back to King Herod, who had bad plans. So they returned home by a different route, their hearts full of joy at having found the greatest treasure of all – Jesus, the newborn King!

Lesson: Just like the wise men, we can seek Jesus with all our hearts and bring Him our best gifts. True wisdom means following God's guidance and being willing to travel far and work hard to find truth.

Interactive Activities:

1. "Star Seekers Adventure":

Create an indoor/outdoor treasure hunt where children:

- Follow star-shaped clues

- Solve simple puzzles
- Find "treasure" to give as gifts
- Learn about seeking Jesus

2. "Wise Men's Journey Map":

Materials needed:

- Large paper or fabric
- Star stickers
- Colored markers
- Pictures of camels and gifts
- Create a giant map showing the wise men's journey

3. "Special Gifts Activity":

Children think about gifts they can give Jesus:

- Kind actions
- Helping others
- Sharing love
- Using talents

Drama and Movement:

1. "Follow the Star":

- One child holds a star

- Others follow as "wise men"
- Navigate simple obstacles
- Find "baby Jesus"

2. "Camel Caravan":

- Form a line like a camel train
- Move slowly and steadily
- Carry pretend gifts
- Sing traveling songs

Songs to Learn:

🎵 The Wise Men's Song 🎵

(To the tune of "Three Blind Mice")

CopyThree wise men, three wise men,

See the bright star, see the bright star,

Following it from afar,

Bringing their gifts to the newborn star,

Gold and frankincense and myrrh,

For the King, for the King!

Craft Corner:

1. "Shining Star Lanterns":

- Clear plastic cups
- Gold paper stars
- Battery tea lights
- String for hanging

2. "Royal Gift Boxes":

- Small boxes
- Gold paint
- Glitter
- Fill with symbols of gifts we can give Jesus

3. "Night Sky Viewers":

- Paper tubes
- Dark paper
- Star stickers
- Learn about following God's guidance

Discussion Questions:

- Why did the wise men travel so far?
- What made their gifts special?
- How can we seek Jesus today?
- What gifts can we bring to Jesus?

Learning Stations:

1. "Star Observatory":

- Learn about stars
- Make constellation cards
- Talk about God's guidance

2. "Gift Workshop":

- Explore the meanings of the three gifts
- Create modern gift equivalents
- Plan ways to give to others

3. "Journey Planning":

- Pack a pretend travel bag
- Learn about determination
- Discuss following God's leading

Family Activities:

1. "Night Sky Watch":

- Go stargazing together
- Talk about the wise men's journey
- Share dreams of serving God

2. "Giving Project":

- Choose gifts for those in need
- Make homemade presents
- Share the joy of giving

Memory Verse Game:

"When they saw the star, they were overjoyed." - Matthew 2:10

(Create star-jumping actions while saying the verse)

Prayer Station:

Create a "Seeker's Prayer Corner":

- Star-shaped prayer cards
- Thankful thoughts
- Requests for guidance

Take-Home Challenges:

Be a "star" for others:

- Show kindness
- Guide people to Jesus
- Share God's love

Give special gifts:

- Help at home

- Be kind to friends
- Share with others

Remember: Like the wise men, we can seek Jesus with our whole hearts and bring Him our very best gifts!

CHAPTER 8: THE FLIGHT TO EGYPT

After the wise men left Bethlehem, something very important happened. One night, while Joseph was sleeping, an angel appeared to him in a dream.

"Quick, Joseph!" the angel said urgently. "Get up! Take Mary and baby Jesus to Egypt. King Herod wants to hurt Jesus. Stay in Egypt until I tell you it's safe to come back."

Joseph woke up right away. Even though it was still dark, he gently woke Mary. "We need to leave," he whispered. "God has warned us to go to Egypt where Jesus will be safe."

Mary didn't ask questions. She trusted God and Joseph's guidance. Quickly and quietly, they packed their most important things. The gifts from the wise men – gold, frankincense, and myrrh – would help them on their journey.

They left while the stars still twinkled in the sky. Baby Jesus slept peacefully in Mary's arms as their donkey carried them toward Egypt. Joseph led the way, watching carefully for any danger.

The journey was long and sometimes difficult. They traveled through places they had never seen before:

Across sandy deserts where the sun was very hot

Through places where palm trees gave them shade

Past pyramids that looked like giant triangles touching the sky

But God was with them every step of the way:

- When they were thirsty, they found water
- When they were tired, they found safe places to rest
- When they needed help, kind people would assist them

In Egypt, they found a new home. It was different from Nazareth – the people spoke a different language, ate different food, and built different kinds of houses.

But Mary and Joseph knew they were exactly where God wanted them to be.

Baby Jesus grew stronger every day. He learned to crawl, then walk, and say His first words in their temporary home. Mary and Joseph waited patiently, trusting God's perfect timing.

Finally, after King Herod died, the angel appeared to Joseph in another dream. "It's safe now," the angel said. "Take Mary and Jesus back to Israel."

Joseph and Mary were happy to return home. Their journey showed them that wherever God leads, He provides and protects. Jesus was safe, just as God had planned!

Lesson: God watches over us and guides us to safety. When we listen and obey quickly like Joseph did, God helps us through uncertain times.

Interactive Activities:

1. "Night Journey Game":

- Create a simple board game
- Move pieces through "safe paths"

- Collect "protection cards"
- Reach "Egypt" safely

2. "Angel's Message Relay":

- Pass whispered messages
- Act quickly on instructions
- Learn about listening and obeying

3. "Safe Journey Obstacle Course":

Set up a gentle obstacle course where children:

- Navigate quietly
- Help each other
- Find safe resting spots
- Reach the "destination"

Creative Learning Stations:

1. "Dream Warning Center":

- Make dream catchers
- Talk about God's messages
- Practice listening skills

2. "Egyptian Adventure":

- Learn about Egypt

- Make paper pyramids
- Try Egyptian snacks
- Draw palm trees

3. "Protection Promises":

- Create a book of Bible verses about God's protection
- Illustrate each promise
- Share stories of feeling safe

Craft Activities:

1. "Journey Journal":

Materials needed:

- Small notebooks
- Colored pencils
- Stickers
- String for binding
- Create a diary like Mary might have kept

2. "Safety Stars":

- Cut out star shapes
- Write ways God protects us
- Make a mobile to hang up

3. "Desert Diorama":

- Shoe box scenes
- Sand (or brown paper)
- Palm trees (pipe cleaners and paper)
- Small figures of the holy family

Songs to Learn:

🎵 God's Protection Song 🎵

(To the tune of "This Little Light of Mine")

CopyGod will keep us safe and sound,

Safe and sound, safe and sound,

God will keep us safe and sound,

He protects us all the way!

Discussion Questions:

- Why did Joseph trust the angel's message?
- How did God help the family on their journey?
- What makes you feel safe?
- How can we trust God when things change?

Role-Play Activities:

1. "Quick Packing":

- Practice deciding what's important
- Work together as a family
- Learn about being prepared

2. "New Places, New Faces":

- Pretend to visit new places
- Practice being brave
- Make new friends

Family Activities:

1. "Safety Scavenger Hunt":

- Find things that keep us safe
- Talk about God's protection
- Make a family safety plan

2. "Trust Walk":

- Lead blindfolded family members
- Practice following instructions
- Build trust together

Prayer Station:

Create a "Protection Prayer Corner":

- Draw outline of a house
- Write prayers inside
- Thank God for keeping us safe

Memory Verse Activities:

"The Lord watches over you." - Psalm 121:5

- Create actions for the verse
- Draw pictures to remember it
- Say it during scary times

Take-Home Challenges:

- Practice quick listening and obeying
- Help others feel safe
- Thank God for protection
- Trust God in new situations

Bedtime Reflection:

- Share feelings about the day
- Remember God's protection
- Pray for safety while sleeping

Extension Activities:

1. "Map Makers":

- Draw the journey to Egypt
- Mark safe places
- Add thank-you notes to God

2. "Protection Promises Box":

- Decorate a special box
- Fill with Bible verses about safety
- Read one when feeling scared

3. "Helping Hands":

- List ways to help others feel safe
- Practice being a good friend
- Share God's love

Remember: Just like God protected baby Jesus and His family, He watches over us too. We can trust Him to guide us and keep us safe!

CHAPTER 9: THE RETURN TO NAZARETH

After their time in Egypt, God sent another angel to Joseph in a dream. "It's safe now," the angel said. "Take Mary and Jesus back to Israel." Joseph was happy to hear this news! But instead of returning to Bethlehem, God guided them to settle in their old hometown of Nazareth.

Little Jesus was walking now, holding Mary's hand as they entered the familiar streets of Nazareth. The air smelled of fresh bread and blooming flowers. Neighbors called out happy greetings, welcoming them home.

Joseph returned to his carpenter's workshop, where the smell of wood shavings filled the air. Jesus loved spending time there, watching His earthly father work. Joseph taught Him how to sand wood until it was smooth and how to choose the right tools for each job.

"Watch carefully, Jesus," Joseph would say, showing Him how to make things with wood. Jesus learned to be patient and careful, just like a good carpenter should be.

Mary taught Jesus too. She helped Him learn the Hebrew letters and told Him stories from the Scriptures. Jesus especially loved hearing about how God had helped their people throughout history.

As Jesus grew, He did many of the same things other children did:

- He helped His parents with chores
- He played with friends in the village
- He went to the synagogue to learn about God
- He asked lots of questions to understand more

But there was something special about Jesus. People noticed how wise He was for His age, and how kind He was to everyone He met. The Bible tells us that "Jesus grew in wisdom and stature, and in favor with God and man."

Life in Nazareth was simple, but it was exactly what God had planned. Every day was preparing Jesus for the important work He would do when He grew up. Just like a seed grows quietly underground before becoming a beautiful plant, Jesus was growing stronger and wiser in His quiet hometown.

Lesson: God prepares us for His plans in ordinary, everyday moments. Just like Jesus learned and grew in Nazareth, we can grow in wisdom and kindness wherever we are.

Interactive Activities:

1. "Growing Wise Garden":

Create a classroom garden where children:

- Plant real seeds
- Watch them grow
- Learn about patience
- Connect growth to learning

2. "Carpenter's Workshop":

Set up a safe woodworking station with:

- Soft wood pieces
- Sandpaper
- Measuring tools
- Adult supervision

3. "Daily Life in Nazareth":

Create stations representing:

- Carpenter's shop
- Market place
- Home activities
- Synagogue learning

Learning Centers:

1. "Wisdom Growing Station":

- Make a growth chart
- Write new things learned
- Share kind actions
- Track achievements

2. "Skills Practice Area":

- Practice writing
- Learn measurements
- Try simple crafts
- Help others learn

Craft Activities:

1. "Growing Tree Book":

Materials needed:

- Paper leaves
- Tree trunk template
- Markers
- String
- Write learning and growing experiences on leaves

2. "Nazareth Village Scene":

- Create a diorama
- Add small figures
- Make tiny tools
- Include daily life details

3. "Jesus' Growing Years Album":

- Draw pictures of Jesus learning
- Write simple stories
- Add Bible verses
- Share family memories

Songs to Learn:

🎵 Growing Like Jesus 🎵

(To the tune of "Jesus Loves Me")

CopyJesus grew up day by day,

Learning, helping on His way,

Being kind in work and play,

Growing wiser every day!

Yes, we can grow too,

Yes, we can grow too,

Yes, we can grow too,

Just like Jesus did!

Discussion Questions:

- What kinds of things did Jesus learn in Nazareth?
- How can we grow in wisdom like Jesus did?
- What do you think Jesus did to help His family?
- How can ordinary days prepare us for God's plans?

Role-Play Activities:

1. "A Day in Nazareth":

- Act out daily tasks

- Practice helping others
- Learn new skills
- Show kindness

2. "Learning Together":

- Share knowledge
- Teach each other
- Practice patience
- Celebrate progress

Family Activities:

1. "Growth Journal":

- Record new skills
- Write down kind acts
- Draw learning moments
- Share family stories

2. "Helping Hands Project":

- Do chores together
- Learn new tasks
- Share responsibilities
- Celebrate cooperation

Prayer Station:

Create a "Growing in Grace Corner":

- Thank God for learning
- Ask for wisdom
- Pray for patience
- Share growth goals

Memory Verse Activities:

"And Jesus grew in wisdom and stature, and in favor with God and man." - Luke 2:52

Create actions

Make art

Write in special ways

Take-Home Challenges:

- Learn something new each day
- Help someone learn
- Practice patience
- Show kindness

Growth Tracking Activities:

1. "Wisdom Wall":

- Post new learning

- Share kind actions
- Celebrate growth
- Encourage others

2. "Skill Builder Cards":

- List new abilities
- Track progress
- Set goals
- Share achievements

3. "Kindness Calendar":

- Plan helpful actions
- Record good deeds
- Notice others' needs
- Celebrate caring

Remember: Just as Jesus grew and learned in Nazareth, God helps us grow and learn every day. Every moment can prepare us for His special plans!

Extension Ideas:

1. "Future Dreams Box":

- Draw future hopes
- Write prayer requests

- Share aspirations
- Trust God's timing

2. "Learning Library":

- Share books
- Tell stories
- Practice reading
- Help others learn

3. "Growth Celebration":

- Share achievements
- Encourage others
- Thank helpers
- Praise God's guidance

CHAPTER 10: THE MEANING OF THE FIRST CHRISTMAS

Once upon a time, in a world that needed hope and love, God gave the most amazing gift ever. It wasn't wrapped in shiny paper or tied with ribbons. It wasn't something you could buy in a store. God's gift was His own Son, Jesus!

Let's think about all the wonderful parts of this special story we've learned:

Remember Mary? She was just a young girl when an angel told her she would be Jesus's mother. Even though she was surprised, she said "yes" to God's plan with a happy heart.

Think about Joseph, who listened to God's messages in his dreams and took such good care of Mary and Jesus. He showed us that being brave means trusting God, even when things seem difficult.

Remember the long journey to Bethlehem? Mary and Joseph traveled so far, and even though there was no room at the inn, God provided a cozy stable for baby Jesus to be born.

The shepherds were watching their sheep when angels filled the sky with light and song! They were the first to hear the good news, teaching us that Jesus came for everybody – not just rich or important people.

And don't forget the wise men, who followed a special star across deserts and mountains just to worship baby Jesus. They brought their very best gifts to honor Him.

But do you know what makes this story so special? It's not just a story that happened long ago – it's a story that changes everything for us today!

You see, Jesus wasn't just any baby. He was God's Son, coming to earth to show us how much God loves us. That's why we celebrate Christmas – to remember this amazing gift of love.

Think about it:

- When you give someone a present, it shows you care about them

- When you help someone, it shows you love them
- When you forgive someone, it shows your heart is full of love

That's exactly what God did, but in the biggest way possible. He gave us Jesus because He loves us so much!

Every part of the Christmas story shows us something special about God's love:

- The angels show us that good news is meant to be shared
- The shepherds show us that everyone is important to God
- The wise men show us that Jesus is worth searching for
- Mary and Joseph show us that God can use ordinary people for extraordinary things

And here's the most wonderful thing: The baby born in Bethlehem grew up to be our Savior, teaching us how to love God and love each other. That's why Christmas isn't just about presents under a tree – it's about the greatest present ever given: God's love for you and me!

Interactive Learning Activities:

1. "Love in Action Calendar":

- Create a special calendar
- Each day, do one act of love
- Share how it made others feel happy

2. "Gift of Love Tree":

- Draw a big tree
- Write ways to show God's love on paper ornaments
- Add new ones as children think of more ideas

3. "Christmas Story Chain":

- Each link represents part of the story
- Connect them all to show how God's plan came together
- Use it to retell the story

Creative Expression Stations:

1. "Thank You Jesus Corner":

- Write thank you notes to Jesus
- Draw pictures of His love

- Make cards to share God's love

2. "Joy Sharing Station":

- Create simple gifts for others
- Write encouraging messages
- Plan ways to help people

Songs to Celebrate:

🎵 The Greatest Gift 🎵

(To the tune of "Jingle Bells")

CopyGod's great love, God's great love,

Sent from heaven above!

Jesus came to show the way,

And fill our hearts with love!

Family Discussion Questions:

- What's your favorite part of the Christmas story?
- How can we share God's love like the angels shared good news?
- What gifts can we give to Jesus by helping others?
- How does knowing God loves us make us feel?

Love in Action Projects:

1. **"Blessing Bags":**

- Fill bags with necessities
- Add encouraging notes
- Share with those in need

2. **"Joy Spreaders":**

- Make Christmas cards
- Visit elderly neighbors
- Share Christmas cookies

Memory Verse Art:

"For God so loved the world that He gave His only Son."
- John 3:16

- Create artwork featuring the verse
- Use bright colors and hearts
- Share what it means to you

Prayer Activities:

1. **"Love Prayer Chain":**

- Write prayers on paper strips
- Connect them together
- Thank God for His love

2. "Circle of Thanks":

- Hold hands in a circle
- Each person thanks God for something
- End with a group hug

Take-Home Challenges:

- Share the Christmas story with someone
- Do something kind each day
- Thank God for His gift of Jesus
- Look for ways to show love

Reflection Corner:

Create a quiet space where children can:

- Think about God's love
- Draw or write their feelings
- Pray quietly
- Plan ways to share love

Family Celebration Ideas:

1. "Love Light Night":

- Light candles safely
- Share favorite parts of Jesus's story

- Sing Christmas songs together

2. "Giving from the Heart":

- Make homemade gifts
- Write loving messages
- Share with others

Remember: Christmas reminds us that God loves us so much, He gave us His Son Jesus. Now we can share that love with everyone we meet!

Final Prayer:

Dear God,

Thank you for loving us so much that you gave us Jesus.

Help us to share Your love with others,

Not just at Christmas, but every day.

Amen.

CONCLUSION

The Christmas Story Lives On

Dear young friends and families,

We've come to the end of our wonderful journey through the Christmas story, but in many ways, this is just the beginning. The story of Jesus' birth that we've explored together is like a beautiful gift that keeps on giving, long after the decorations are put away and the holiday season is over.

More Than Just One Day

You know how excited you get on Christmas morning, rushing to open your presents? Well, the gift that God gave us on that very first Christmas is even more amazing than anything we could find under a tree. It's a gift of love so big that it changed the whole world!

Remember how we learned about:

- Mary and Joseph's faith and trust in God's plan?
- The shepherds who heard the angels sing and rushed to see baby Jesus?

- The Wise Men who traveled so far, following a special star?
- And most importantly, the tiny baby born in a humble stable who was actually God's own Son?

Each part of this story teaches us something special about God's love and how we can live our lives in a way that makes Him happy.

Lessons from the Christmas Story

Let's think about some of the big ideas we can take away from the Christmas story:

- **God's love is for everyone**: Just like Jesus was born in a simple stable, not a fancy palace, God's love is for all people, no matter who they are or where they come from.
- **Big things can come in small packages**: Baby Jesus looked like any other newborn, but He was the Savior of the world! This reminds us that we should never underestimate anyone, including ourselves.

- **Faith can help us do amazing things**: Mary and Joseph trusted God even when things were scary or confusing. We can have that kind of faith too!
- **It's important to share good news**: The shepherds and Wise Men couldn't keep the miracle of Jesus' birth to themselves – they had to tell others! We can share God's love with people around us too.
- **Giving is better than receiving**: God gave us the best gift ever – His Son. This teaches us that the joy of giving to others is even greater than getting presents ourselves.

Christmas All Year Round

Now, here's a fun question to think about: What if we could keep Christmas in our hearts all year long? I don't mean putting up a Christmas tree in July (although that might be fun!). I'm talking about keeping the spirit of Christmas – the love, kindness, and joy – alive every single day.

Here are some ways we can do that:

- **Show kindness**: Remember how the innkeeper found a place for Mary and Joseph? We can look for ways to help others, even when it's not easy.

- **Practice gratitude**: The shepherds and Wise Men were so thankful to see baby Jesus. We can remember to thank God for all the good things in our lives, big and small.

- **Share with others**: The Wise Men brought gifts to Jesus. We can share what we have with people who need help, not just at Christmas but all year.

- **Forgive**: Jesus came to forgive our mistakes. We can practice forgiving others when they hurt our feelings or make mistakes.

- **Spread joy**: The angels sang with joy when Jesus was born. We can try to bring happiness to others through our words and actions.

A Special Mission for You

Do you know what's really exciting? The Christmas story isn't over – it's still happening today! How? Well, every time we choose to love others, to be kind, to forgive, or to help someone in need, we're continuing the story that began in Bethlehem so long ago.

You have a special part to play in this ongoing story. Every day, you have chances to show God's love to the people around you. It might be as simple as sharing your toys with a friend, helping your parents with chores without being asked, or being nice to someone at school who seems lonely.

These might seem like small things, but remember – the greatest story ever told started with a tiny baby in a manger. Your small acts of love and kindness can make a big difference in the world!

A Prayer for All Seasons

As we finish our time together with this Christmas story, let's say a little prayer. You can use this prayer any time of year when you want to remember the special gift of Jesus:

Dear God,

Thank you for loving us so much that you sent Jesus to be born as a little baby.

Help us to remember the joy of Christmas all year long.

Show us ways to share your love with others every day.

Thank you for the gift of Jesus, the best present ever!

Amen.

The Story Continues with You

So, my young friends, as you close this book, remember that the story of Christmas is a timeless reminder of God's love, and we are called to share that love with others. Whether it's the middle of summer or a cold winter's night, the magic of Christmas can live in your heart always.

Every time you're kind to someone, every time you share, every time you choose love over anger, you're keeping the Christmas story alive. You're showing the world that the baby born in Bethlehem so long ago still changes lives today.

May the joy, peace, and love of Christmas be with you always, lighting up your life and the lives of those around you. And remember, just like the star that led the Wise Men to Jesus, you too can be a bright light in the world, leading others to know God's amazing love!

Merry Christmas today and every day!

AUTHOR'S NOTE

A Journey of Faith and Wonder

Dear Readers, Parents, and Guardians,

As I sit down to write this note to you, my heart is filled with warmth and gratitude. The journey of creating this "Bible Christmas Story for Kids" has been more than just a writing project—it has been a profound spiritual experience that has rekindled my own childlike wonder at the miracle of Christmas.

A Personal Connection

I still remember the first time I heard the Christmas story as a child. It was a cold December evening, and my family had gathered around our living room fireplace. As my grandmother's gentle voice narrated the tale of Mary, Joseph, and the birth of baby Jesus, I felt as if I was right there in Bethlehem, witnessing this extraordinary event unfold.

That childhood experience planted a seed of faith in my heart that has grown stronger with each passing year. Now, as an adult and an author, I find myself returning to this timeless story again and again, always discovering new layers of meaning and inspiration.

The Journey of Writing This Book

When I embarked on the journey of writing this book, I thought I knew the Christmas story inside and out. After all, I had heard it countless times, read numerous versions, and even participated in many Nativity plays (I was a shepherd three years in a row!). However, as I delved deeper into the narrative, carefully considering how to present it to young readers, I found myself experiencing the wonder of Christmas anew.

I spent hours imagining what it must have been like for Mary to receive the angel's message, for Joseph to trust in God's plan despite his initial doubts, for the shepherds to witness the heavenly choir, and for the Wise Men to embark on their long journey following the star. With each scene I wrote, I felt as if I was walking alongside these biblical figures, sharing in their joys, fears, and ultimate triumph.

This process of deep reflection and imagination has profoundly deepened my understanding of Jesus's birth. I've come to appreciate even more the humility of God choosing to enter our world as a vulnerable infant, the faith required of all those involved in the nativity story, and the revolutionary message of hope and love that this event brought to the world.

A Gift to be Shared

As I wrote each page of this book, I was constantly reminded that the story of Jesus's birth is indeed a gift to the world. It's a narrative that has the power to touch hearts, inspire kindness, and bring people together in a spirit of love and unity. By sharing this story with you, dear readers, I feel that I am participating in keeping the true spirit of Christmas alive.

My hope is that as you read this book with your children or grandchildren, you will feel the same sense of awe and wonder that I experienced while writing it. I pray that the words and images will spark meaningful conversations in your family about faith, love, and the true meaning of Christmas.

An Invitation to Families

To the parents, grandparents, and guardians reading this note, I want to extend a special invitation. Reading this Christmas story together as a family can be more than just a holiday tradition—it can be a powerful tool for fostering a deeper faith and creating lasting memories.

Here are a few suggestions for making the most of your family reading time:

- **Create a cozy atmosphere**: Choose a comfortable spot, maybe with some soft Christmas lights or candles, to help set a special mood for story time.
- **Take turns reading**: If your children are old enough, let them read parts of the story. This can help them feel more engaged and connected to the narrative.
- **Pause for reflection**: After each section, take a moment to discuss what you've read. Ask your children what they think about the characters'

actions or how they might have felt in similar situations.

- **Connect to your own lives:** Help your children relate the story to their own experiences. For example, talk about times when they've had to be brave like Mary, or trust in God like Joseph.
- **Encourage questions:** Children often have insightful and sometimes challenging questions about faith. Welcome these questions as opportunities for growth and learning together.
- **Extend the story:** Consider acting out scenes from the story, creating artwork inspired by it, or finding ways to apply its lessons in your daily lives.

Remember, the goal isn't perfect understanding, but rather opening hearts to the wonder of God's love as shown through the birth of Jesus.

A Journey That Continues

As you close this book and put it back on the shelf, know that the story doesn't end there. The message of Christmas—God's incredible love for humanity—is one that we're invited to carry with us throughout the year.

My prayer is that this retelling of the Christmas story will plant seeds of faith, hope, and love in the hearts of your children, just as my grandmother's storytelling did for me so many years ago. May these seeds grow and flourish, inspiring a lifelong journey of faith and a desire to share God's love with others.

Thank you for allowing me to be a small part of your family's Christmas celebration. It has been an honor and a joy to share this precious story with you.

Wishing you and your loved ones a Christmas filled with wonder, love, and the peace that comes from knowing the greatest gift of all—Jesus Christ.

With heartfelt gratitude and Christmas blessings,

[SPARK CRAFTER]

P.S. I'd love to hear how this book has impacted your family! If you'd like to share your experiences or have any questions, please feel free to reach out to me through my website or social media channels. Let's keep the conversation—and the Christmas spirit—going all year round!

Made in the USA
Columbia, SC
21 December 2024

50363231R00054